The Sound of Your Voice Series #1

True Value

The Joseph Story

By Bob Nolan

The Sound of Your Voice Series #1

True Value
The Joseph Story

By Bob Nolan

ISBN 978-1-61529-043-7

Vision Publishing
1672 Main St. E 109
Ramona, CA 92065
1-800-9-VISION
www.booksbyvision.com

All rights reserved worldwide. No part of this book may be reproduced in any manner whatsoever without written permission of the author except brief quotations embodied in critical articles or reviews.

Recommendations

"Bob Nolan is a true prophetic minister of God. Instantly, powerfully, he is lifted into insight and perception regarding people, churches, meetings, and nations. His prophetic words bring hope and healing for those to whom he ministers. Bob's life has been refined in the fire, producing brokenness within him, thus he yields to the Spirit and God's life flows into others. Anyone hearing Bob teach is moved by his skillful, passionate handling of the Bible. As he opens the drama of Scripture, his insightful gifting gives it intensity, making it relevant for the times."

Evangelist Mary Ruth Meredith
By My Spirit, Inc., San Marcos, CA

"Bob Nolan will come to your congregation as a friend, and that is no understatement. His simple yet profoundly prophetic style will move you to God, not a personality, and keep your heart and mind before the Lord. We celebrate his gift, and love his ministry."

Pastor Jon David Kendall
North Point Church, San Diego, CA

"Bob combines the experience of a seasoned elder with the passion of a child in Father's lap. As a result, the saints are equipped through prophetic coaching to become ambassadors of Jesus Christ. The Holy Spirit moves. True, loving coaching surfaces. Spiritual, loving warriors are raised up. It's my pleasure to recommend Bob Nolan to you without reservation."

Pastor Jeff Daly
Jesus Christ Fellowship, Clear Lake, CA

"Brothers in America – In every seminar with Roberto we have received great spiritual blessing. Every pastor attending these seminars has expressed gratitude and satisfaction for what he has accomplished through his ministry. Much of the vision we now have is the result of your helping send brother Roberto to Honduras and supporting him. Gracias!"

Pastor Panchito Enamorado
Iglesia Filadelfia, Santa Barbara, Honduras

"In times of need or in times of trial, God's people can expect to hear HIS voice through Bob. And God truly speaks to His people in cross-culture settings effectively through Bob - even when he doesn't speak the language. He speaks HIS language."

Pastor Chris Lung
Living Streams Chinese Christian Church, Carlsbad, CA

The Sound of Your Voice Series #1

Table of Contents

Forward 6

Preface... 8

Chapter 1: True Value.. 11

Chapter 2: Got Fruit?.. 21

Chapter 3: The New Emmanuel... 31

Chapter 4: Hidden Treasures 41

Chapter 5: The Gift of Empathy 47

Chapter 6: Outrageous! Forgiveness....................................... 53

Chapter 7: Joseph's Destiny... 61

Forward

I have always enjoyed the life of Joseph. I like dreamers, and of course, Joseph is known as a type of Christ in that he saved his family from famine and forgave his disgruntled brothers. Joseph was not perfect as was Christ, which is why he is only a type. The fact is, I never thought he was that smart, at least in the beginning of his journey. He was naïve at best to tell his father and older siblings his joy that they would bow down to him. You do have to be careful with whom you share your dreams.

In spite of his weaknesses and trials, there are many lessons learned from this extraordinary biblical character. Yet, having read much on the life of Joseph, I really was blessed and surprised to see a unique treatment of this young man with the coat of many colors, in the writing of a unique gift to the body of Christ, Bob Nolan.

Bob, in a most dynamic style, illustrates through Joseph's life how the Lord develops his called people to not only hear the voice of God, but to echo it. As Brother Nolan states, "He (God) wanted to develop an ambassador He could trust, a son with whom He could co-operate." God's heart is for us to speak for him, to represent him—but first we must know the One we represent, or we will inevitably represent Him inadequately. What a thought! Being is more important than doing in God's economy. The emphasis of so many in the body of Christ today is doing all the right things, which is fine. But the expectation is that *doing the right thing* will somehow produce the character of God in a young man or woman. God, however, is more interested in relationship than all we might ever do for Him. Before doing, we must know the Lord.

Bob also states, "they all had opinions—even Heavenly words and dreams—but there was a language school they had to attend. To interpret God, to represent God, to actually sound like God took more than religious training or vocabulary or technique. Learning to appreciate God's friendship in the crucible of misunderstandings, mistakes, and betrayals developed an empathy and a Sound in their mouths that would help many people hear their gracious Father. God spends abundant effort and eternal exertion to train us in His values. God can build puppets. He'd rather train an ambassador." Ambassadors have a primary responsibility of speaking only what the King or President or Prime Minister instructs them to, not as parrots, but as loyal emmisaries who know what to say and when to say it. They know the heart of the leader for whom they speak.

God trusts us as His people, and He has invested His most precious gift into us, with every expectation that fruitfulness will come from our lives for the benefit of all. Finally, Bob states; "It is one thing to quote God, even accurately. It is quite another thing to sound like Him. The Holy Spirit is God involved with us. The Holy Spirit is the new Emmanuel for the New Covenant Age in which we live." And, by the empowerment of Spirit in our lives, we can learn to speak, and the sound of our voice will echo the Voice of our heavenly Father.

This book is not ordinary in form or content…it is dynamic and life changing. I cannot recommend both the author and the book more highly. It will help the reader to understand more fully just how much the Father loves us and how his desire is to partner with us. Through the illustrated life of Joseph, you the reader will see how much the Father favors you to be the sound of His voice, as you step out and be the sound of your own voice.

Dr. Stan DeKoven

President and Founder of Vision International University and International Training and Education Network (ITEN)

Preface

A favorite philosopher of mine, Yogi Berra, once said, "You can see a lot by just observing." Yogi had a firm grasp on the obvious. But, ain't it the truth? And maybe it ain't so obvious. Maybe the *obvious* needs to be reconsidered.

Learning to teach, preach, counsel, prophesy, and generally speak for God takes more than learning technique or memorizing Scriptures. Observing—with interest—how the Spirit of God developed some of His finest ambassadors is part of any spokesperson's education. Anybody can quote God, but few sound like Him.

The theory in this series of booklets is that you can see a lot by just observing. You can learn a lot by considering. You can accomplish a lot by believing. Joseph is our first *observable* candidate in this sound-of-your-voice series. Here was a favored, gifted, smart, sincere young man with no trace of dishonesty or politics in his soul. He had dreams and words from God. But God was interested in more than a puppet He could *use*. He wanted to develop an ambassador He could trust, a son with whom He could co-operate. Joseph had words, but God wanted to add a Sound. A Sound from Heaven that could impact people and nations beyond the mere conveyance of words. So Joseph was sent to God's Heavenly Language School, to learn to interpret, not just translate. To obtain a Sound, not just words.

There is a clamor in the air for prophetic training and how-to manuals on the delivery of words from God. This series is neither about technique or how to. It is about the way our Heavenly Father develops a son who can represent the Family Business. His methods may seem severe—because sometimes, they are. The stakes are high, so the training is strict.

The likes of Joseph, Peter, Jacob, David, Jeremiah and others were all "called" while young, immature, and quite sincere. They all had opinions—and even Heavenly words and dreams—but there was a language school they all had to attend. To interpret God, to represent God, to actually *sound* like God took more than religious training or vocabulary or technique. Learning to appreciate God's friendship in the crucible of misunderstandings, mistakes, and betrayals developed an empathy and a Sound in their mouths that would help many people hear their gracious Father. The tuition for that language school is steep. The benefit of the Diploma is priceless.

The Holy Spirit usually inspires stories without a moral. He just tells the tale and lets the reader figure out who are the good guys and the bad guys. To "get" God's stories, you have to figure them out. Consider. Remember. See it in your own life.

Just observe. And you will see a lot.

(Hint: Read Genesis 37-50. Make your own observations. Then, see if mine make any sense.)

The Sound of Your Voice Series #1

Chapter 1: True Value

"I rejoice at Your Word, as one who finds great treasure." Psalm 119.162

Why do you go to work, attend a meeting, engage in conversation, or invest in a venture? Because you believe it's worth it. You'll obtain something from it. It has value. That value may be monetary or it may mean some kind of advantage. You may expect an immediate dividend from your investment, or perhaps it's a seed outlay for some future benefit. But no one does anything for nothing. It's human nature—even God's nature—to expect a return, even if it's for someone else. To appreciate. To appraise. To understand worth.

Good value starts with "a fair return or equivalent in money, goods, or services for something exchanged" (Webster's). Of course, we always want a little better than fair value, but fair is a good start. When a retailer can offer goods or services at a great value on a special sale, he can expect a crowd. Value attracts. Good value entices. **True Value is from Heaven.**

Value means more than how much something cost, which means expense. I may pay ten dollars for a souvenir that, to me, represents something worth more than ten dollars. Its *value* to me surpasses its *cost*. On the other hand, like Jesus' Kingdom parable about the Pearl of Great Price, I may have to purchase a whole field—very expensive—to get the Pearl I value so much. Cost is what you have to pay. Value is in the eye of the beholder.

God the Appraiser

In a curious verse of Scripture, the Psalmist says that "Precious (valuable, worthy, rare—Hebrew: *yakar*) in the eyes of the Lord is the death of His saints" (Psalm 116.15). Since the Lord owns all the cattle and all the gold and all the nations, we might suppose He is so wealthy, that He values nothing. But the opposite is true—He values things like no one else. Most wealthy people value their resources, and invest carefully. An artist values her skill. Whatever your profession is, because you have paid a price to practice it, you value it. You expect to be paid. A doctor gets paid for what he gave up in order to obtain his skills. He lost his life for years to be able to give a diagnosis that takes only a moment to express.

God is the one, ultimate Appraiser of what is worth-y. True valu*ing* originates in Him. His saints are precious to Him, and when one dies, God feels the loss. That Hebrew word, yakar, is used many times in the Old Testament, and always signifies something rare, like a gem—or priceless, like a life.

What is the most *expensive* thing in the universe? No matter what planet or culture you're from, the answer is simple—whatever *cost* the most. Ask the Thief on the cross next to Jesus. Ask a blood-washed saint. Ask God the Father. He spent His Son to obtain that immeasurably costly thing—*forgiveness*. Not for Himself, but for the likes of us. God understood the cost. He decided the expense was worth it. He spent. He obtained.

What is the most *valuable* thing in the universe? The answer here is also simple. Whatever *means* the most. Ask the Devil. He told Jesus that he would give Him 'all the kingdoms of this world' for that one priceless thing—a moment of Worship. Back in Heaven, Lucifer had (apparently) led worship before the very Throne of God (Isaiah 14). But he let it go to his head. He saw all the other Heavenly Hosts worshiping and said, "I want that for myself. I want to be like the Most High." He was deceived, but right about one thing—Worship is very valuable. But worship is only for Him who is Worthy of it, and only God can sit in that Seat. Satan wanted it, and still wants it. He wanted something that he could not handle even if he got it.

A Word from God—Priceless

The prophetic ministry is a most valuable grace that the Savior has given to the church for precious human beings. Though it is a grace-gift poured out to us from Heaven, like other endowments, it comes at great cost. The story of every Bible prophet/ ambassador is one of God spending long seasons and radical energy on building His own Thoughts and Character into that person's soul. At the end of their lives, words from the likes of Joseph, Moses, Ruth, or Paul were of unspeakable value. Their lives had been sifted, their motives refined, and their words were Heavenly.

How valuable is a Word from God?

How valuable is a Word from God? How precious is it to hear from the Everlasting One? How deeply can you explore the ages of eternity to begin to appreciate an Eternal Word from Heaven? "Oh, the depth of the riches and wisdom and knowledge of God! How unfathomable (inscrutable, unsearchable) are His judgments and decisions! And how untraceable, mysterious, and undiscoverable are His ways (His methods, His paths)! For who has known the mind of the Lord and who has understood His thoughts, or who has ever been His counselor? Or who has first given God anything that he might be paid back or that he could claim repayment?" (Romans 11:33-35, Amplified).

God has higher motives than to simply drop His Words in the mouth of a prophetic person, like a ventriloquist puts words in the mouth of a puppet. He wants to co-operate with us in speaking to precious (yakar) souls He desires to address and encourage. His intention is to train us so that we are as careful with our words as He is with His. Because when God works on a servant and takes His message and burns it into his / her soul it is to burn His very Heart into that prophetic minister. There is great risk and expense on God's account. Think of it—He entrusts us with Words, and the delivery of those Words, that can change a person for eternity. That change can be good or bad! . . much depends on the sound and delivery of those words.

So as the genuine prophetic minister pours out words of the Spirit to other human beings, he is not simply parroting out words he has heard from heaven. He is cooperating with Him to deliver His Heart to human beings He loves and with whom He wants to communicate. That minister is delivering the Heart and Secrets of Heaven into souls with eternal value. These Words themselves are more valuable than can be appraised with mere human words. They are priceless. Yakar.

Expensive Ointment

But though they are price-*less* in terms of value, there is a *cost* to carry and deliver these eternal Words of encouragement. One of the ways we describe the phenomenon of God speaking through His servants in prophetic ways is the analogy of the "anointing." The idea came from the desert kindness that hospitable hosts would show to their guests. They would take a precious dab or two of olive oil and rubbing it onto the dry skin of a weary visitor. This expensive oil would also be used to heal wounds and became symbolic of making a friend feel at home. Over the years, the kind act took on deeper significance, as prophets would use the oil to anoint kings, expressing approval, appointment, and ability from Heaven. The olive oil revealed the precious-*ness* of God's approbation.

How valuable was that oil? How precious is the anointing of God to elevate mere men into the holy arena of speaking and sounding like God? What is the value? What does it cost?

One day, on the way to a prophetic training meeting, the teacher stopped at the store and purchased a small bottle of olive oil. When the meeting started, he passed out a slip of paper to each person with a line for their name and a line for a price. He said, "Write down what you think the bottle of olive oil cost at the store. The closest guesser will take the bottle home." After the teaching time, he went over the papers and yes, there was a winner. After giving him the bottle the teacher asked, "So now we know what I paid for it. But what is it really worth? I know what it cost in dollars and cents, but if you really want to know the cost, you'll have to ask the olive. Only he knows. After all, he was crushed so you could enjoy the oil."

Isn't that the way it is with the anointing of the Lord? Words from Heaven are given and received and blessed and considered and enjoyed. But someone paid a price for that precious oil. Someone's life was exacted for the ointment that comforted a soul and extended the Kingdom on earth, as it is in Heaven. Something—someone—was crushed. What is the true value of the anointing? Those that walk with God in the anointing, in ever deepening appreciation of what it costs to be obedient and to serve—they begin to know the cost of wearing the oil of the Holy Spirit.

We know that salvation is free and that only Jesus' precious (yakar) blood can remove our sins. But to walk in God's anointing—closely to Him where His words of true worth can come to human beings and actually change their lives, encouraging desperate people to live another day, and apprehend minds and hearts for the Kingdom of God—this is costly. What is the value of the anointing? God knows. Ask the olive.

"Carrying Precious Seed"

Psalm 126.6

Speaking valuable words

What is the *value* of a Word from God? What do Words from Heaven actually accomplish in the recipient? What can these Heavenly Sounds do in a human being, in a family, in a church, in a community, even in a nation if they are delivered by the timing and grace of the Holy Spirit? Not only the specific words, but the Sound. The Sound Jesus made was full of *both* grace and truth.

God's Words become even more precious when they come through a human being to another human being, because that messenger puts the reality of a face and life to Words from Heaven. When those words come through a life that has been touched by the life and intense heat of God, it gives profound poignancy to the Message from Above.

Here's a great question you might ask someone who is able to deliver these precious words—"What did you have to go through to obtain those treasures? What kind of fire and trial and aloneness did you experience to be able to speak like this to desperate persons?" Words of hope that have come from a processed servant of the Eternal God are inestimable in their value. Like the rarest wine that has been aged in a cellar, one sip tells you that it is not cheap or hastily produced.

If you've heard from God, or delivered a Word to someone from Him, you know that it's not a matter of money! "CD of a Sunday sermon, $5. A leather Bible, $59.95. A Word from the Mouth of God, Priceless." God is profuse and elaborate with His Words. Yet, He never wastes even one. Everything He says is pertinent, relevant, timely, and timeless. He warns us about 'every careless word' we speak, because His character is so alert to how He spends His words. A single word from God can accomplish more in a moment than ten thousand dollars' worth of counseling. David was talking *value* when he wrote, "I rejoice at Your Word as one who finds great treasure" (Psalm 119:162).

God is generous and yet fastidious about distributing His Words. Who can say what it cost God to know what He knows, to comfort, to command, and to direct His children by His Words? His Supremacy and Ownership of all things does not mean that He does not feel the expense of what He so generously gives. When a philanthropist gives to a charitable foundation, he carefully considers and weighs the worth. He 'feels' the cost, but decides it's worth it for the sake of the cause. Believers agree that God is generous. How could we call Him generous if all His giving of words and provisions were cost-less to Him? And what does it cost

Him in terms of time and effort to actually burn those Words into our souls?

Thinking like God Thinks

An essential aspect of the prophetic ministry is to understand what God values and what He does not. Take note of both the quality and quantity of time Jesus spent explaining to His apprentices what really mattered, and what did not. For example, the religious leaders put a lot of stock in how hands and utensils were washed before eating, as though it was essential to righteousness (see Matthew 15.2-8). But Jesus said that washing etiquette is not nearly as valuable to God as it was to those Pharisees. He explained, in contrast, that mercy was quite precious to His Father.

The Master constantly, by word and action, demonstrated the worth of people who were desperate for survival in this life and for salvation in the next. Individuals wanted God's righteousness and friendship in their lives. Jesus called them *the poor in spirit*. He put a value on them by telling us to expend effort and time upon them. "You got it for free," He said. "Give it away for free." (Matthew 10.8)

Job said, "the Lord gives, and the Lord takes away." God was in deep conversation with Job, explaining to him what was truly valuable and what wasn't. His ultimate goal was not to bring Job into poverty, because He did restore to Job the blessings of this world he had previously enjoyed. God did not take away what was truly valuable—*He removed the temporary, temporarily —* to show Job what was *eternally* precious. Job then saw what was important for eternity and for other lives. He said, "I had heard about You before, but now I see You with my own eyes" (Job 42:5-6).

> ***God spends abundant effort and eternal exertion to train us in His values.***

Another prophet had said, "My ways are not your ways, neither are My thoughts your thoughts"—My values are not your values (Isaiah 55.8-10). God spends abundant effort and eternal exertion to train us in His values. This is fundamental as well as upper division Kingdom teaching, especially for His prophetic servants. It is basic truth, it is deeper truth. Embracing His values means a serious review of our old priorities. How can He trust a person who does not share His own appreciation of what He thinks is good, or bad?

Trusted with His Word

Like Job, Jeremiah had been in his own desperate situation. He had been promised (Jeremiah 1) that he would be a prophet to nations. God told the young minister that He had intimately known him before he had been formed in his mother's womb. When Jeremiah accepted that call, he thought it would be smooth sailing to addressing the nations. But only a few years into his ministry, he found himself slandered, accused, and the target of government-sponsored persecution. He was charged with treason, deprived of privileges, and actually thrown into a septic tank. A slave had to rescue him. He radically questioned God, saying, "Lord, you deceived me, and I was deceived; I am ridiculed all day long, everyone mocks me. Whenever I speak, I cry out . . . the word of the LORD has brought me insult and reproach all day long" (Jeremiah 20:7-8). But the Lord showed him there was a journey to be walked between the Promise and the fulfillment. God had not forgotten the promises, nor had He neglected them. He didn't want a puppet, He was developing a spokesman. Ha! A press secretary He could trust.

What could be better than trusting Him? Only one thing—when He trusts you.

Jeremiah was learning God's Priorities. He was given the clearest God-statement about the most essential ingredient of prophetic ministry. "If you will separate the precious—the valuable—from the worthless, you shall be as My mouth" (Jeremiah 15.19). God wasn't talking about quoting Scripture or even having a convicting message. He said that if Jeremiah would appreciate the difference between what was valuable and what wasn't, he would be God's Mouth on earth. Then, God could *trust him* to be His mouthpiece, His direct emissary. This is what the Lord is looking for to entrust us with the prophetic ministry. Who could *de*preciate the value of trusting in the Lord with all your heart? What could be better than trusting Him? Only one thing—*when He trusts you.* When His priorities and values become yours, He can begin to trust you with His precious things—His Word, His people, His heart.

God spoke this to Jeremiah in Old Testament days, long before Christ came. It was long before the Holy Spirit was poured over the Body of Christ, and long before the present Prophetic ministry was given to extend the Gospel. Now He is saying that same Scripture to men and women, boys and girls all over the earth. He is anxious to entrust more, not fewer, persons with His valuable Words for other human beings whom He loves. If you understand the True Values of Heaven, you will be His mouth. "My Character will be your character, my Heart will be your heart. The words that come out of your mouth will be the Words that come out of My mouth. I will back you up." A oneness, a fellowship with God beyond what we have yet asked or even thought. "You will see as I see, and love as I love, and speak as I speak." This is authentic prophetic ministry. This is making the Sound of His Voice. This is how the sound of *your* voice becomes the same Sound as His Voice.

One person can say the same words as another. But the one who is influenced by God begins to sound like God. When desperate humans walk away from the person who's been with God they say, "Didn't my heart burn when I talked with him?" You are spoken to, why not listen?

God can build puppets. He'd rather train an ambassador.

The Sound of Your Voice Series #1

Chapter 2: Got Fruit?

Joseph is a fruitful vine, a fruitful vine near a well, whose branches climb over the wall. With bitterness the archers attacked him; they shot at him with hostility. But his bow remained steady, his strong arms stayed limber, because of the hand of the Mighty One of Jacob, because of the Shepherd, the Rock of Israel. **Genesis 49:22-24**

On his deathbed, Jacob spoke this blessing to his lost-but-found son, Joseph. After so many years of hard trials and loss, the old patriarch enjoyed his last few years in the presence of his sons and grandchildren, and God came through on His promise that 'Joseph's own hand will close your eyes.'

Joseph. For centuries teachers and theologians have taught us that this young man more typified the Savior than any other person in Scripture. He is known as a type of Christ, which is someone in the Bible who reminds us of Jesus before Jesus arrived as a human being. Reading the life of Joseph (Genesis 37-50) makes its own teaching and suggests its own morals. The messianic character of his person is unmistakable, as old divines have found at least one hundred ways that his life parallels that of our Lord. Joseph. Forgotten, forlorn, and made of no reputation. Loved. Preferred. Hated. Sold. Accused. The Dreamer. The Interpreter. The Governor. A man of sorrows, acquainted with grief. The great Forgiver.

In the Bible, fruitful is another word for valuable.

There's no use trying to appraise the value God places on any human being. To search the depths of His feelings and the worth He places on every person made in His image is impossible and inestimable. Let's just say that every human being is supremely valuable to his Maker. You and Abraham Lincoln and Judas Iscariot were all born with that priceless worth.

But not every human being is valuable to other human beings. That's why God gets involved. They're already meaningful to Him. He wants to make them worth something to other people, so that His Dream of covering the planet with His glory can be realized. So that their influence improves families and cultures. **So that they don't only quote God, they actually sound like Him and speak with His manner.**

Often, God develops people-value in His sons in what the Bible calls the furnace of affliction. Betrayals. Misunderstandings. Jealousies. Rip-offs. Reputation damage. Loss. When Joseph—the subject of this little book—was denied everything he was promised and about which he dreamed, the only comfort he had was, "but the Lord was with him."

God wasn't with Joseph as a curious, impervious bystander. He was with him so that Joseph's sorrows would not be wasted. He was with him to change him from gifted, to a Gift. From a dreamer, to His Dream. From making a noise, to speaking a Sound from Heaven. When the Scripture says that God is with you, it's not that He's just there. It means He is involved.

It is one thing to quote God, even accurately. It is quite another thing to sound like Him.

Joseph's value—for other people—increased because he walked through his twenty-two-year-long death valley. He discovered, obtained, and carried treasures found only in dark places. At seventeen, he was special. His dreams were accurate and the favor of his father was upon him, as well as God's. But though he had dreams and words from Heaven, he did not necessarily have the heart or voice of God worked into his soul. He was a good boy. He loved his father. He worked hard. He had good insights and meaningful words. But he did not yet sound like God. It is one thing to quote God, even accurately. It is quite another thing to sound like Him.

In Jesus' day, many religious leaders had the Scriptures memorized. They could quote the words of God with precision. Jesus spoke the same words. But the people said, "No one ever spoke like this man." Jesus had more than words to quote. He had the Sound of Heaven. That is God's dream, that we would Sound like Him, and make that Sound all over the planet. God's furnace is made to produce ambassadors.

Early Days, Formative Seasons

Joseph was born while his father was still working at Laban's, hundreds of miles east of the homeland and Esau's wrath from which Jacob had fled. As a little boy, he enjoyed the extraordinary affection of his father, being the firstborn of beloved Rachel. He could remember the day when his father suddenly announced to the family that their twenty-year welcome had been worn out at uncle Laban's. They would be saddling up before dawn to begin the long westward journey back home to see Grandpa Isaac. Weeks later, close to home, he experienced panic in the family's camp as news came that Esau, the angry uncle, was on his way with four hundred armed men. The next morning Dad came back to camp, limping, but with the glory and peace of God all over his face. Perhaps, when they finally made it back to Bethel, Jacob stopped and showed Joseph where he had slept and dreamed about the stairway to heaven. What profound impressions were imprinted in the mind of this favored son.

When Joseph was just a teenager, his dad knew there was something special about him, even though the youngster had irritated the whole family with his dreams. His ten big brothers were overcome with jealousy over the favoritism shown him. They relieved their bitterness by selling the boy to a band of slave-traders headed for Egypt. Over the next twenty-two years, God wove together an astounding tapestry of injustice, intrigue, and restoration as He prepared the 'human pillars' of the twelve tribes of Israel. Jacob was heart-broken, Joseph was mistreated, and the ten brothers lived with a conscience more burdened than we can imagine. BUT God, in his amazing grace and mercy, showed once again that He is the unseen Hero of every Bible story.

And God is the un-seen hero of your life, and every life He intends to employ in covering the land with His Glory. That Dream is "Christ in you, the Hope of Glory." There is no Plan B. He puts the treasure in jars of clay. Not to be a puppet used by a Celestial Ventriloquist, but an ambassador sent by a Dad-King. Not just with quoted words, but with the Sound of His Voice in your mouth. People will say of you, hours or days or months after you've spoken the Kindness of Heaven upon them, "Didn't our hearts burn when he spoke to us?" **They'll know it was you. But they'll know that it was Someone Else, too.**

The Hidden Source

The most significant statement explaining Joseph's life and value was repeated over and again in Genesis, then quoted by Stephen in his martyr's sermon in Acts 7.9, 'But God was with him.' Surely, early in his life Joseph began thirsting and searching for the unseen God of his father and grandfathers. The jealousy and misunderstandings he felt from his brothers only served to push him deeper into a divine trust. In a polygamous family with four mothers vying for favors for their sons, the ground was fertile for envy. It was long before he was thrown into the pit that this young man began to be 'a vine planted by a well.' Father Jacob, on his deathbed, perceived that the Well had been Joseph's hidden strength. Because of the Well, Joseph would save a family, and a nation. He would have more than dry words. He would develop a Sound with water from Heaven. His exquisite pain would forge a strength and a sound within him that would help nations. No human being could endure Joseph's trial without help from above. He was undoubtedly a suicide candidate. But he was connected to a Well. Unseen, but deep and real.

We westerners don't appreciate wells. Pipes bring water to our homes from man-made reservoirs. We turn the handle and the water magically appears. But a well is a deep, unseen, created source, greatly appreciated by desert dwellers. Joseph had to learn to obtain his life and rest without anything being piped into his soul from outside reserves. God wanted to build a man who would depend only on his Well, his unseen-but-never-ending Source. He often hides His life-giving power from the casual, those who are not thirsty. Finding a well requires some searching and some digging. Joseph became a vine whose roots had to go deep into the waters of God. Later, a great Man would call it "a well springing up into eternal life." "Hey Joseph, got fruit?" Yes.

It seems Joseph may have had some lack-of-maturity problems that aggravated his troubles, but were also part of the plan of God. Certainly, the dreams he had about his brothers bowing to him were from God. But Joseph! Why would you share such dreams with them when they were already irritated by your father's preference for you? They knew you had given a bad report about them to dad. On top of it all, you visit them in the sheep-fields wearing that coat. Joseph! Wake up and smell the coffee...get a clue, Joseph!... you are casting your pearls before swine, and they're going to turn on you and tear you to pieces. Oh, Joseph. You are the gift that keeps on irritating.

There may be no record of sin in Joseph, but there was plenty of youthful naiveté. Time and again he would flaunt his favor or express his dreams. His favor and dreams were from God. He was remarkable. He could speak with clarity. But to his family he was a noisy clamor. His sound was fingernails-on-a-blackboard. He was not a false prophet, but certainly an immature one. Like how most of us "gifted" folks start the journey.

And everyone knew Joseph was gifted. Dreams. Insights. Favor. It was all over him. But, at least in his family, he was not considered a gift. Imagine walking into a Thanksgiving dinner with your family and announcing that all your brothers and sisters— even your mom and dad—would one day bow down to you.

Joseph's visions were finally proven to be from God. He was gifted. But the gift-wrapping was obnoxious. God had no intention of un-gifting Joseph. Neither does He intend to un-gift you because of mistakes or immaturity. But there was a needed preparation to take his gifted-ness, and turn him into a Gift from Heaven. And as long as it would take, the Preparer had the time and the love and the determination to get the job done. Welcome to the Kingdom of our Dad.

...God's language school produced a Sound in Joseph that could change a king.

Even the best Words from Heaven can cause disturbance. Sometimes, our Heavenly Dad can express warnings or even an occasional rebuke. But the purpose of those Words always point to encouragement, comfort, and building up. In a word, Peace. In his youth, Joseph did not always deliver Peace with his words. His dreams—sincere and favored as he was—provoked jealousy and insecurity in his family. But if you check out the end of the story, Joseph's trials produced a peace in his soul and in his words. He said to Pharaoh, "God will give you an answer of Peace." He never lost his gifted-ness. But God's language school produced a Sound in Joseph that could change a king. His abilities, and ours, are given from Heaven. But that's not enough. God wants to elevate our soul and our sound to Heaven, so they can make eternal impact.

Never assume that anyone's lack of maturity—including your own—is a dis-qualifier for employment in the Lord's Dream. Joseph's impulsive behavior even became a tool for God to get him where He wanted him. How many of God's choicest sons learned the Sound of God's Voice as they spilled milk all over the Kingdom floor. Dad is not nearly as impatient with us as we are with each other. Ask Jacob.

During national crises in Biblical times, God sent alarm into his leaders and people to provoke them to seek Him with all their hearts (e.g., see 2 Chronicles 20). The eternal heroes were those who set their faces to find God in the middle of trouble, and turned the hearts of the people to Him. Each had a well from which to draw—a well that had been dug during their own personal dry times. When this happened, calamities were averted, enemies fled, and the nation prospered. It is powerful, yet merely natural, to be unified against a common enemy. A common enemy makes for strange bedfellows — like Democrats and Republicans. But when the enemy cannot be defeated by natural means, even with patriotic unity, people will turn to those who have a well inside their lives...those who have been involved with God, and He with them.

Maybe a period of pain and trial pushed you toward God in a way that nothing else would have. Maybe it's for such a time as this that you have been called to live in your nation, or your neighborhood, or your home. Maybe your cries to God have created a well inside you for people who had no need of God – until now. Maybe your own pain has made you ready to stop, to look, to listen, to empathize with those who are ready to look for the only Strength worth having. God works His deepest wells into those who trust Him during the darkest times.

One day, after Jesus returned to heaven, leaving the spiritual climate of earth forever changed, apostles Peter and John were dragged into a Jerusalem courtroom to explain by what authority they were preaching and healing people. No one could deny the miracles and that people had been helped, but the jealous priests and lawyers felt they had to shut the preachers up. The erudite rulers were stunned, wondering how such uneducated men could have such power. And the only thing they really knew about these coarse fishermen was that they had been with Jesus (Acts 4.13). Who had the real authority then? Who had a well from which to draw? The same ones with the real authority now – those who have been with Jesus and have the goods for thirsty, hurting people. Now, those are eternal heroes. Isaiah 50.4

Trusting God in the Detours

> *God's dream for Joseph was loftier than simply developing his character.*

Only God knows how ready we are to be employed by Him in His prescribed plan and to be able to truly represent Him on this planet. That was His purpose for Joseph, as it is for you and me. He will take our mistakes, our sins, and even our long-term misguided tours and weave them together for good to them that love Him, to them that are called according to His purpose. **Whether Joseph was wrong or dumb or even in sin is not the point.** God had a plan in His eternal purpose that was bigger than Joseph's problems. He even used his troubles to orchestrate a story that is an astounding picture of Redemption Story. As we shall see in the coming pages, Joseph was developed—through years of agony—into an ambassador who not only knew the right things to say, but how to say them. He learned obedience. He learned forgiveness. He learned the Sound of Heaven through the things that he suffered.

God's dream for Joseph was loftier than simply developing his character. As the story unfolds, you see that He had His own Glory and the benefit of many other people in mind. God had to do a work so thorough in Joseph's heart and character that he would not have even a hint of revenge or even self-vindication in him. What a profound picture of the Hand of God working simultaneously with the choices and sins of men. Did Joseph's brothers send him to Egypt, or did God? Yes. In the Genesis story, there is no mention of God having had anything to do with this family crime. Yes, the brothers did it. But in Psalm 105, "'He sent a man before them — Joseph—who was sold as a slave" Ps.105.17. So, God did it. The Great Orchestrator was at work again, behind the scenes, preparing a man and a nation to reconcile a family of rascals, and to make them ready to be the patriarchs of His chosen people. In the end, Joseph knew what to say, and how to say it. When you are mistreated by people, God is involved behind the scenes. You may be in ambassador-training.

Please take note. God sent Joseph. If that was all we read, it sounds like a promotion. And it was a promotion. But just like the promises of promotion to other prophets, apostles, intercessors and the like, the promotion involved delays, detours, and un-speakable trials. So whether you speak or receive a cool prophetic word about the Lord doing some promoting . . . understand that it probably will not be a slam-dunk. Our gracious Savior will prepare His sons to handle the responsibility of a position before He places them on that very hot seat.

A character study on this young man's life would lead us to say that God was making him holy. But this is not a character study—it's a Preparation Study. How does God take a lump of clay—a mess—and turn it into a beautiful soul? As special (holy) as God wanted Joseph to be, the preparation was intended for him to be helpful for other people. To help a family. To help a king. To help a nation, and to "save many people alive" (Genesis 50.20).

What a portrait of Jesus. Sent by his father on an errand of kindness to his brothers. He came to seek his own, but his own did not receive him. 'This is the heir, father's favorite. Let's get rid of him and get the inheritance for ourselves!' His own brothers hated him because he spoke what he saw. He found himself in a pit, but wound up on a throne. But Jesus was less self-conscious about His throne than He was about helping others come into His Kingdom. At the end of the day, the same was true about Joseph. At the end of your life, God's intention is that the same will be true about you.

When I was first married, I was even more self-absorbed than I am now! Oh, I loved Jesus and perhaps a few friends. But my heart was so small. I had little capacity to love like God loves, and even less capacity for empathy. God had a remedy—He started giving me kids. Late night feedings, early morning diaper changes, inconvenient moments. These normal duties forced me to make small but frequent investments into someone other than myself. Over time, Jesus' strange words began to make sense to me, "Where your treasure (value) is, there is where your heart will be, also" Matthew 6.21. Now, God's heart is still quite a bit larger than my own (oh yes). But because I had to invest the treasure of my time into someone else at my own inconvenience, my heart began to grow. Out of selfishness. Out of carelessness. Out of my own life and holiness, into the importance of other people. Whether it's kids or prison or the injustice of betrayal, God will prepare His ambassadors to speak and to love and to act in order to save and bless other people.

Like the Savior of whom Joseph was a "type," he had to learn obedience through the huge hassles he suffered. There is no record of Joseph ever being dis-obedient, and neither was Jesus. But Obedience is more than avoiding dis-obedience. It is learning to hear a Voice and actively, even happily responding to it. So it is with a son in whom Dad is pleased. It takes years to learn to trust Him and get the dis-obedience out. To trust Him with all my heart and not lean on my own understanding. Then, something even better happens. Better than trusting God? Yes. **It's when He starts trusting you.** With a word. With a life. With a position. Maybe with a nation of hungry people.

In the end, all things did work together for good in the lives of Joseph and the whole family. God is building a testimony in His kids' lives that no matter what we have to walk through, no matter who meant evil toward us, the Lord meant it for good. And that good will spread His Dream all over the planet and all over many people.

Oh I hope I'm not nagging. It's one thing to be called. It's another thing to be prepared and ready. Meanwhile, before you attain that calling, remember your influence can still be valuable, even while you're in prison.

Chapter 3: The New Emmanuel

"I will ask the Father, and He will give you another Helper, that He may be with you forever" John 14:16

At creation, before God had started His beautification plan for the earth, *'the Spirit of God was hovering over the face of the waters. Then God said, Let there be...'* A giant principle of God was set into the universe that has startling implications for our lives. The Holy Spirit hovers over a situation or a life that is formless and void (i.e., a hopeless mess!) and waits for Father God's timing. As soon as the Word of the Lord comes, He springs into action and makes awesome, wonderful things happen. The Holy Spirit is *God involved with us*. The Holy Spirit is the new Emmanuel for the New Covenant Age in which we live.

> **The Holy Spirit is God involved with us. The Holy Spirit is the new Emmanuel...**

'God with us' means much more than the doctrine of the *omnipresence of God*. You can believe deep in your heart that 'God is everywhere' and still feel totally alone – and *be* totally alone. You've heard of being lonely in a crowd? You can also feel lonely even if you're convinced that God is standing right next to you. Emmanuel is more than simply God in the room. Emmanuel is *God involved with you*. God was not just there observing Joseph, He was involved. His Hand was always on the thermostat of Joseph's furnace of affliction. The old Gospel song says that He walks with me and He talks with me and He tells me I am His own. Now that's Emmanuel. God with me. God for me. God involved with the turns and decisions of my life. God on my side.

When Jesus-Emmanuel showed up down here in the real world with us, He demonstrated His commitment to radical involvement with us. He paid the ultimate price to convince us that He personally understands our weaknesses and fears. He was *'tempted in every way that we were tempted'* and so is able to be with us as an empathetic participant in life. He is not my heavenly observer. He is my ever-present Coach. He is my Friend. So whether He is discipling me, blessing me or allowing unexplainable trials to test my faith, He is with me. Involved with me.

What good is the revelation of God *with* us if He is not *involved* with us? The strange doctrine of Deism says that God created everything, but then stood back and let the universe spin on its own like a top whose string He pulled. Pantheism goes further and says that everything *is* God. But there is no Emmanuel for deists and pantheists. No God who walks and talks with them, or leads them in the way which they should go. Even Christians, in the heat of trials and the uncertainties of life can wonder where God went. Jesus Himself went through the ultimate test of faith when He cried, *'My God, why have You forsaken Me?'* Because He went through all that He went through, He could say with power and authority, *'I will NEVER leave you, or forsake you.'* It's true. Stop and believe it right now– He will never, for any reason, by any means, under any circumstances, at any time, through any pressure, by whatever threats of darkness, ever, ever leave you. Emmanuel is involved with you now and constantly and forever. Ask Joseph.

Fathers and mothers in the Spirit experience an exquisite kind of alone-ness.

To drive home the reality of Jesus' permanent involvement in your life, He can – and often does – put us in circumstances where we are forsaken of human companionship. That strange and awful sense of deprivation and loneliness is sometimes the needed recipe for our turning to fellowship with God as our only source of strength and comfort. The great men of the Bible spent poignant and sometimes long seasons of alone-ness so they could truly fellowship with God and to be able to bring God to others. Abraham alone to sacrifice his son. Jacob left alone at the River Jabbok to wrestle with God. Moses alone for 40 years in the Midian desert. John alone on the Isle of Patmos to see what only God could show him. Joseph alone for twenty-two years so he could make the sound of God to his mean brothers. I call this the Discipline of the Patriarchs. Fathers and mothers in the Spirit experience an exquisite kind of alone-ness. Think of it. Who does God the Father have to look up to? Even Jesus had His Father to whom He could look up. Father is alone. To experience alone-with-Emmanuel is to have genuine fellowship with God. He may get you isolated to cure you of loneliness. He knows what He's doing. Isolation is one of the key disciplines for all patriarchs, prophets, and true friends of God. Pain, with gain.

>Vindication is good…integrity is good…
>success is good…justice is good…
>the bad guys getting caught is good…*but*

God's Timing is Everything!

> *'He has made everything beautiful in its time. Also He has put eternity in their hearts, except that no one can find out the work that God does from beginning to end.'* Ecclesiastes 3:11

How do you suppose our friend Joseph felt about all his dreams and promises while slaving in the Egyptian muddle he was in? Being sold into slavery wasn't just unpleasant and scary, it was the *opposite* of what God had shown him—the antithesis of his destiny. Just like at Creation, things appeared to be a hopeless mess. "Lord, did you just walk away from the work You started?" But the Holy Spirit was hovering, waiting over Joseph's fragile, rejected life. He was waiting for—you guessed it—God's timing.

And the timing God uses to initiate rescues and provisions and destiny for you is Divinely impeccable. New Covenant prophetic ministry sees and speaks about the Glory of God, beyond the obvious mess. In Joseph, God saw a beautiful soul long before he became Prime Minister of Egypt.

God has a way of starting every project with nothing, except a Word. He doesn't call Home Depot to see if there's enough lumber or Wells Fargo to qualify for a loan. That includes everything from Creation to the tiniest details of your life, and Joseph's. *In the beginning was the Word ....through Him all things were made; without Him nothing was made that has been made. Jn 1.1,3* God wanted Joseph to learn that His promises would be accomplished with no help from him, including his own vindication. To the natural eye, the road to the fulfillment of God's plans often looks like the wrong direction. But the Holy Spirit is hovering over your mess (!) knowing that Father's timing *always* works, *always* succeeds, *always* is best. *Until the **time** that Joseph's word was fulfilled, the Word of God tested him. Ps 105.19.* Do you have an old prophecy stuck in the back of your bottom drawer that you gave up on? Pull it out and re-believe it! The only thing that matters is that God said it. The Lord wants us to know that it is His love and power that will get the job done in us and through us at exactly the right time.

> *There may be un-heavenly voices against your own dreams.*

There was a conspiracy of hate against Joseph. Perhaps you have felt that same kind of conspiracy against the life and dreams embedded in your heart from the Spirit of God who has continued to hover over your messes. Was not Jesus the very Representation of the Dream of God for the whole earth? He came to repair the broken Dream. His Dad's Dream that the Land would be filled with His Glory, His Personality. Like the #1 Son, Joseph was taken out because people were jealous of the dreamer and his dreams. *"Look, this dreamer is coming! Come, let us kill him and cast him into some pit; and we shall say, 'Some wild beast has devoured him.' We shall see what will become of his dreams!"* (Genesis 37:19-20). Same thing when the Savior hung on the tree—*"He saved others, let him save himself. Let him come down from the cross."* There may be un-heavenly voices against your own dreams. "Who do you think you are?" But keep dreaming the Dream of God. There will be friends who see you by the Spirit. Like Jacob, who was irritated by his favorite son's dreams, but pondered them in his heart. "There's something about that boy. God is planting him by a well."

Sometimes, and with unspeakable sadness, it can be those whom you thought were friends, and even your family, that most painfully reject you out of jealousy. Ask Jesus.

It's easy to theorize about the timing of God, but it takes real spiritual power to help desperate people see it. At first, Creation was a mess. Joseph's life was a mess. Your friend's life may be a mess. Joseph faced innumerable trials in Egypt, though only the major ones are recorded in Scripture. Who can imagine the dark nights of the soul he experienced in over twenty years of slavery and prison, through no fault of his own? His ordeal is a divine study in the timing of Emmanuel. After regaining some sense of dignity and hope in his first Egyptian job, he became the head steward in Captain Potiphar's house. His master had noticed that *'the Lord was with him' Gen 39.3.* Maybe the trial is over! Maybe now I'll have some rest for my soul and be able to buy a ticket for a caravan back home.

But the worst was yet to come. Potiphar's wife had problems of her own, and "day after day" she plagued the poor boy with seducing speeches and ploys. This was a prolonged, nagging kind of trial. *Joseph, it's not really a trial till it lasts a while!* You know the story (Ge 39). When she couldn't have her way with God's young man, she threw a tantrum, screamed Rape!—and the hero wound up in prison. False accusation and judgment is its own peculiar kind of test, especially when you cannot defend yourself.

It wasn't yet **time** for Joseph to be exalted. (I have always believed that Potiphar did not really believe his wife's story. If he did, Joseph would have had worse than jail.)

While in prison, Joseph kept working faithfully and even the warden noticed that *'God had prospered him.'* He was actually put in charge of all the other prisoners! People *noticed* Joseph's behavior—and people notice yours. God has a way of putting persons around you—during your most difficult times and when all you can think about is your pain—that are watching your every move. Yes, Joseph (and you) are being watched. Potiphar and the warden and others knew instinctively that this young man was under enormous pressure, but they noticed that "Someone" was helping him. When the butler and baker showed up in the same prison, they were watching this abused young man. And finally, when his hour of deliverance did come, even Pharaoh paid attention—Pharaoh said to his servants, *"Can we find such a one as this, a man in whom is the Spirit of God?" Genesis 41:38.*

> *There are responsibilities and moments of influence waiting beyond the horizon for you.*

Your behavior and words during times of injustice are being noticed. You may be *unwittingly prophesying* with your life. After the trial is over, people who watched you will remember that your faith is real. What kind of *sound* do you make when surrounded by injustice? You are being watched, often by those who seem to ignore you.

When Pharaoh's butler and baker were thrown in with him and shared their strange dreams, Joseph thought he saw a way out. After interpreting his dream he said to the butler, *'But when all goes well with you, remember me and show me kindness; mention me to Pharaoh and get me out of this prison.' Gen 40:14* Oh boy! I'm going to get out of here! After all, God helps those who help themselves, right?

'Yet the butler did not remember Joseph, but forgot him Ge 40.23 Joseph thought he'd help God, but Emmanuel's timing had not yet come, and He would not be rushed. Two more years in the prison pressure cooker were needed for Joseph to be ready for the amazing responsibilities God had for him. There are responsibilities and moments of influence waiting beyond the horizon for you. Keep your hand on the plow. Keep helping. Keep kindness. Bless what is Beautiful. Have you ever tried to help God by rushing things just a bit? (Of course you haven't. But now you'll be able to warn other people about it, yes?) If *God's time* has not yet come, it's a *good time* to trust and wait.

As Yogi said, "It ain't over till it's over." But, When It's Over, It's Over

But after two years, God's time had come. Pharaoh had some of the weirdest dreams of his life, and his best dream experts couldn't give a satisfying interpretation. There was a divine stamp on these dreams, and Pharaoh knew it. Suddenly, God Himself stung the butler's conscience and he remembered Joseph…with no help from Joseph! He remembered everything, down to the details. What if the butler had told Pharaoh about Joseph's abilities when Joseph had wanted him to? Pharaoh would not have cared, because he had no need of a Hebrew slave-prisoner telling him anything. But because God delayed the timing, the butler had a testimony about Joseph *just when Pharaoh needed it.* Pharaoh's desperation made him open to God's chosen vessel, whereas before, he did not even know that Joseph existed. God's word, God's dealings, and God's timing had put a humility and a confidence into Joseph that made him

> *The treasures of wisdom you have obtained will be required, and those in need of them will find you.*

ready to stand even before a king. Does the Lord know what He's doing, or what?

Want to hear a secret about Emmanuel's timing? You'll never figure it out. Because this whole Christianity deal you're in is about a faith relationship. But when the Divine Time has come, there is a Pharaoh who will call for you. This "pharaoh" may not be a king or anyone you may expect—but you will be called. You will be needed. The treasures of wisdom you have obtained will be required, and those in need of them will find you. God has been behind the scenes, orchestrating famines and upheavals that will necessitate *your* involvement. Whether it's a man or a business or a family or a political system, there will be a pharaoh that will seek you out for an "answer of peace," and you will deliver—because you waited for the Lord.

When God's timing has come, things can change more quickly than you even wanted. Joseph didn't know it, but God was preparing Pharaoh to be ready to hear him. *God's timing was the critical factor.* Suddenly, everyone knew where Joseph was and everyone was ready to be his friend. Pharaoh immediately called Joseph out of prison. Here was a despised Hebrew slave doing what Egypt's best wise men could not do—He heard Pharaoh's dreams, interpreted them, and gave advice that would shape the destiny of a nation. Pharaoh was so moved, that he made Joseph his prime minister—even though it would be fourteen more years before the interpretations could be confirmed as accurate. *'Where else can we find such a man, in whom is the Spirit of God?'* Are you in a dungeon? Do you feel quite forgotten? God is preparing you to give someone an answer of peace from the Spirit.

How can such a powerful impression be made so quickly? Only because of God's preparation and timing. *'The king sent and released him, the ruler let him go free. He made him head of his house, and ruler of all his possessions'* Psalm 105.21 Truly, *'no one can figure out the work God is doing between the beginning and the end.'* But could there be a pleasant surprise in store for you if you'll just wait patiently for Emmanuel?   Oh, yeah. *Isaiah 64.4*

The Sound of Your Voice Series #1

Chapter 4: Hidden Treasures

"I will give you the treasures of darkness, and hidden riches of secret places "Isaiah 45:3

What an advantage it is to know the future. To remove the uncertainty from the outcome of wars, championship games, and romantic relationships would take a lot of stress out of life. You could make a lot of money if you knew the future, predicting Super Bowl victories or the direction of the DOW. But wouldn't life be dull? Nevertheless, there is much pressure on us to prognosticate or "have the faith" to know what will happen at the end of our ordeals.

There are priceless treasures in the Kingdom of God that are only found in difficult places and circumstances, which always involve UN-certainty. We insist on knowing the outcome of our trials. But if we knew the outcome, it wouldn't really be a trial. We could plan, adjust, and have the comfort of knowing when it would end. But the heroes of the Bible and of modern life are those who keep on keepin' on even in the face of failure, disaster, or betrayal.

The Valley of UN-Certainty
The Treasures of Heaven's Timing

Two of my favorite heroes in the Bible are Joseph and David. (We consider David in another booklet in this series.) Both of them went through unspeakably dark periods in their lives when every dream and every promise from God seemed like a bad joke. Reality was not just different than the words God had spoken to them – reality was the direct opposite of what God had promised. It's easy for us to look back and say, "Well, everything worked out OK for them, so what's the problem? Of course they should have kept the faith." But Joseph and David didn't know the outcome of their stories until God delivered them. Joseph was 22 years in Egypt after his brothers threw him into a pit and sold him. David was chased through the Judean countryside for 7 years by evil King Saul before his dark valley was finished. Joseph never knew God's end-game until Emmanuel's timing had run its course. Neither do you. But count on it—it's good.

"Until God's promise to Joseph really happened, that very promise tested him," Psalm 105.19. When God promises you victory, success, effectiveness, and fulfillment, expect an adventure. The process seems the direct opposite of the promise. You'll have to navigate lots of little hills and valleys before you make it to the top of the main mountain. God has to dig a big hole before He makes a lake. That was the purpose of Joseph's pit—to make him a refreshing drink for his brothers, who were themselves desperate for God's kindness and forgiveness. Most of the treasures you find in the valley of uncertainty will benefit other people even more than yourself. But isn't that the Kingdom way? Jesus-Emmanuel turned water into wine. Spirit-Emmanuel will turn your pit into a well.

Anybody can quote God, but few sound like Him.

May I continue to hammer on this? Joseph—like many of us—had many good words in his mouth, but he had to attend God's language school to be able to truly interpret Him. To sound like Him. To have His Voice, not just His words. Here I go again. Anybody can quote God, but few sound like Him.

The most important promise of God to remember while you're in tough, dark circumstances is that there are treasures to be found there. "The hidden riches of secret places." Have you ever been in a cave and lost your flashlight? Every step is an adventure. You wonder if you're going to step into a hole or onto a snake! You hear noises that really aren't there. It's so dark that you might as well close your eyes. But God says, "Keep the eyes of your heart open when you're in the darkest cave of disappointment or despair. I have secret treasures for you to find there, and only there. I will give you the treasures of darkness, and the hidden riches of secret places" Isaiah 45.3. Those are the things God gives to His servants who've walked through dark, painful valleys with Him, so they can minister His Hope-ful promises to those who are weary and desperate. There are treasures that will glow just bright enough for you to see and obtain, if you will just look and reach for them. When you finally get out of the cave, those rocks will turn out to be priceless jewels of encouragement for other weary travelers.

When God has you in a valley of darkness, even despair, you don't have many choices. He has removed the direction or outcome of your situation from your own control. You can't get out. The pressure, darkness, thirst, and hopelessness of the place bears down on your soul. Your only real choices are on the inside. To panic, or to trust. To get mad, or to humble yourself before God and men. To run from God, or to Him. When I panic, I close my eyes, hold my breath, run like crazy, and think only of myself. I will probably miss anything of value there is to see. But when I trust – even when I cannot know how things will end up – God can point out treasures to me that I would not otherwise have found. His treasures glow in the dark! God's most valuable treasures are eternal, extremely practical, and absolutely priceless. You will gather some for yourself, some for others, and some to just offer back to God in worship. But you must calm down and trust Him. The worst case scenario is to pass through the darkness and miss what you could have obtained. As much as you hate the valley of uncertainty, it is the gift of your Father. There is no guarantee you will be back in the same valley again.

"My son, if you receive my words, And treasure my commands within you, So that you incline your ear to wisdom, And apply your heart to understanding; Yes, if you cry out for discernment, And lift up your voice for understanding, If you seek her as silver, And search for her as for hidden treasures; Then you will understand the fear of the Lord, And find the knowledge of God. For the Lord gives wisdom; From His mouth come knowledge and understanding" Proverbs 2:1-6.

Maybe another way to put it: When you find yourself in a position that feels like a prison, pay attention to the blessings and comforts from Heaven, even the little ones. They'll shine like the sun for others when you're finally released.

Good Reason for a Long, Hard Season

There are certain Kingdom treasures found only when you're totally dependent on God. Most of us only get "totally dependent" when we can no longer depend on ourselves. He has you there for a reason. The valley of uncertainty – when you don't know the outcome of your difficulties – is a place where great treasures are found. Trust. Forgiveness. Wisdom. Empathy. Understanding. Patience. Love. Did you know that these are treasures of the Kingdom? **Before you went through this valley of dreadful threats and UN-certainty, it was easier to come to quick conclusions about others and their problems.** But now, you're a little slower on the draw. A little less judgmental. A little more apt to wait for God's perspective on a person or situation. One of the prophetic testimonies about Jesus was – "And He shall make Him of quick understanding in the fear of the Lord: and He shall not judge after the sight of His eyes, neither reprove after the hearing of His ears: But with righteousness shall He judge the poor, and reprove with equity for the meek of the earth" Isaiah 11:3-4.

Good Friday and Easter Sunday serve to remind us that Jesus suffered immeasurably and "was tempted in every way that we have been tempted, only without sinning." He can totally relate to any dark moment in your life or emotion. When Jesus cried out, "God, why have You forsaken Me?"— He was in the ultimate valley of UN-certainty. Every devil in Hell and every chief in Jerusalem were accusing Him – "Come down from the cross if You're the Son of God! He saved others, but He can't save Himself." Jesus is known as the Pioneer of our faith. He has walked through every dark valley we could even imagine. "Yea, though I walk through the valley of the shadow of death" – now that's uncertainty – "I will fear no evil, for Thou art with me"

Psalm 23. Jesus Himself had to trust by faith that His Father would raise Him from the dead and bring Him back to the glory of heaven.

Jesus experienced and felt everything we feel, only more deeply and without giving in to panic. The night before He died, He told His disciples that He was so depressed that He thought He would die (Mark 14.34). Imagine the shame that was poured out on His Soul as He hung on the tree, all our guilt upon His kind Soul as God punished our sins upon Him. (Read Isaiah 53). He knew total accusation, total rejection, total sorrow, total loss, total disappointment, total betrayal, and even total UN-certainty about the outcome. "My God, why have You forsaken Me?" He knew Father's plan, but had to completely trust Him to carry it out. Jesus could only control His own heart as He suffered from enemies and even from friends. The dreadful, dark valley Jesus walked through was the place He obtained the greatest treasure of all – our eternal lives. What kept Him from quitting in the middle of all that gross emotion was the same thing that will keep you and me from quitting – He kept trusting in the goodness of His Dad. He kept obeying. He kept His peace with God. What an Amigo we have in Jesus.

Are you, even right now, in a place of radical UN-certainty and hanging by a thread in your finances, key relationships, or concern for your children? Are the promises of God sounding like they were made to someone other than you? Stop the panic. Open your eyes. Check out the treasures. Gather them for yourself and for others.

God was with Joseph. God is with you. His timing is perfect. That's what you need certainty about. Period.   Ephesians 1.17-18

The Sound of Your Voice Series #1

Chapter 5: *The Gift of Empathy*

God will take someone who has been on top of the world and bring him low to understand that God's Kingdom and ways are not of this world. Isn't that what happened to the King Himself? "How He left the realms of Glory, bore the cross of Calvary . . . He left His Father's throne above, emptied Himself of all but love, and bled for Adam's helpless race." The hymns and stories are endless.

Moses had to be as high as a prince to feel and appreciate the shame of being as low as a slave. The slaves could not appreciate Moses' sympathy at first, because they saw Moses as a prince and as an enemy. So God had to take Moses to Midian so his sympathy could develop into empathy. The gift of empathy is bigger than the gift of sympathy. Empathy takes longer than sympathy. Sympathy is in the mind, empathy is in the spirit. Sympathy has sentiment, empathy has power. **Empathy is more valuable than sympathy.**

> *Empathy is more valuable than sympathy.*

> *Webster's: em-pa-thy - the experiencing <u>as one's own</u> the feelings of another*

Paul had the same problem. He was a prince, a Pharisee of Pharisees, blameless in the Law, a Hebrew of Hebrews, and the golden boy of the Sanhedrin. He was a biblical, philosophical, forensic genius. He could intellectually sympathize with all of Israel. Fourteen years in the desert developed Paul's sympathy into empathy. Now, God would show him all the things he had to suffer so he could touch otherwise untouchable people – like his own people. The people who persecuted Joseph the most, Moses the most, Jesus the most, and Paul the most were the people who needed them the most. But they all had to learn obedience and empathy through things they had to suffer. Hebrews 5.8. At the end of the story, the man who had the greatest right to attack his enemies became the purveyor of Forgiveness from Heaven.

It was the discipline of the patriarchs. To be a patriarch is to be a parent is to have responsibility for people is to have to feel alone at the top. (Now that is a run-on sentence!) God the Father is alone at the Top. To really get to know Him, you may have to experience alone-ness. When Abraham had to stand alone sacrificing his only son (Genesis 22), he was beginning to empathize with God the Father. Not everyone wants that kind of fellowship. But it's the best. Empathy with God. It's the kind you'll remember forever.

Fellowship with God the Father

Who needs you the most? He may persecute you the most. But he is only a blade of grass, a first fruit that represents a harvest that you are called to reap. And you will reap. Your sickle has a name written on it. The name written on your sickle is empathy. The name written on your forehead is compassion. You may have to give your life for people who have hated you, so they can be saved in the end. That is fellowship with God.

Paul's greatest persecutors were the people whom he loved the most, and the people with whom he could relate the most. He couldn't believe that the Jews rejected him. He was experiencing the fellowship of Jesus, who came to His own, and they received Him not. Paul's words about the Jews (Ro. 9-11) were a prophecy of empathy for those who wanted to kill him. The arrogant gentiles criticize the Jews and ignore Paul's words about them. Ishmael persecuted Isaac. Egypt persecuted Moses. The Jews persecuted Paul. The false shepherds persecuted the Good Shepherd. Businessmen persecute marketplace ministers. The flesh persecutes the spirit. But the persecuted will save the persecutors, because their sympathy turned into empathy.

Moses had his anger. Paul had his thorn. Jacob had his bad hip. Joseph had to lose everything. You have your family dysfunction. All God's servants have a limp so that the glory stays with Jesus. Even Jesus learned obedience through the things that He suffered. Empathy has power. Persuasion power. Insight power. Intercession power. Door-opening power. Because sympathy makes you cry, but empathy gets under people and lifts them up.

"Trust in the Lord with all your heart, and do not lean on your own understanding" Prov 3.5. That's one of everyone's favorite scriptures. Trusting the Lord while you're going through horrendous trials is the hallmark of God's best ambassadors. But there's something even better. What? Better than trusting the Lord? Yes, here I go again. It's when the Lord trusts you. Because His compassion and empathy have so infiltrated your soul that He can trust you with His treasures for other people.

Jesus defined friendship when He said, "You are My friends, because I have told you everything that My Father told Me" (John 15.15). Friends tell each other their deepest secrets and trust them with their most treasured thoughts. God is your Friend. Are you His? Can He trust you with secrets about people He loves? Can He give you empathy on top of your sympathy? Can He count on you to speak with His manner? His Sound? Every Christian is given the words of the Bible, but when the Holy Spirit gives you words for broken people, or for the church, or for a neighbor going through unspeakable trials; you are being trusted as God's friend. You are His ambassador. You are the body of Christ. Empathy is power that connected Jesus to the worst of sinners and it will do the same for desperate people to whom He sends you.

> *Desperate people need a friend, not a philosopher – empathy, not sympathy.*

What would it be like to be such a friend of God that He didn't even want to do something without telling you? *"And the Lord said, 'Shall I hide from Abraham My friend what I am going to do?'" Gen 18:17, Amplified.* The fact is, GOD, the Master, does nothing without first telling his best friends the whole story. The only problem is that God makes you ready to handle it, first. *Because "confidence in an unfaithful servant in times of trouble is like a broken tooth, and a dislocated foot" Prov 25.19.* Desperate people need a friend, not a philosopher – empathy, not sympathy. Job's friends had great philosophy, but they had no clue. So, instead of walking a mile in his shoes, they shamed Job.

I don't doubt that when Joseph spoke his dreams to his family, he did it with a smile. There may not have been an ounce of meanness in his voice or even in his spirit. He may have shared those visions with a motive to encourage them all. But he had no empathy. He did not have a clue about putting himself in their shoes, and what it was like for them to hear those dreams. He may have had care. He may have had sympathy. Just like I have had in my previous preacher days. But God wanted to take Joseph—and you and me—to the land of empathy, where we can actually feel the heart, and pain, and dreams of other people. To invite them in to the compassionate love of God our Father. Empathy is better than sympathy. Being gifted is not nearly as meaningful as becoming a Gift.

> *Jesus is not offended at your anger, but giving Him the silent treatment will prolong the ordeal.*

You may be angry with the Lord, but keep the conversation going. Jeremiah got angry. He said, "O Lord, You deceived me, and I was deceived; I am ridiculed all day long; everyone mocks me. The word of the Lord has brought me insult and reproach all day long" (Jer 20:7-8). Jesus is not offended at your anger, but giving Him the silent treatment will prolong the ordeal. Ask me.

"We don't have a priest who is out of touch with our reality. He's been through weakness and testing, experienced it all — all but the sin. So let's walk right up to him and get what he is so ready to give. Take the mercy, accept the help." Hebrews 4:15, The Message.

The Sound of Your Voice Series #1

Chapter 6: *Outrageous! Forgiveness*

'Mercy triumphs over judgment'   James 2.13

Imagine being Joseph in Pharaoh's court. An hour ago, you were serving a hopeless life sentence for attempted rape on an Egyptian official's wife. The top of your career was to be in charge of a bunch of other prisoners. With no hope of parole or appeal, your efforts to find an advocate failed with the butler who forgot about you. But suddenly, you're in the presence of the most powerful man on earth, with his full attention on you and your analysis of his dreams. You're promoted to the top of the *Dream Team* – Egypt's best interpretation wizards! Your words are so impressive that Pharaoh reaches out with his staff and anoints you as the new prime minister. Quite a day.

And even in the presence of a Pharaoh, Joseph was able to walk in empathy. Not that Pharaoh needed anything material or cultural from the young Hebrew. But Pharaoh was disturbed by dreams that even his dream-team could not interpret. He had no peace. Joseph had no need to show off, and he had already lost everything. Like they sang in the late 60's, *Freedom's just another word for 'nothin' left to lose.* All he had was all that Pharaoh needed—*an answer of Peace. Peace from God. Peace with God.* Though this Regent had no knowledge of the true, living God, he knew in his soul that he had come into the presence of the Divine. *"Where else are we going to find someone in whom dwells the Spirit of God?"* Somehow, even high level human beings know when God really does show up.

Behind the scenes God has been at work, preparing people, building bridges, and opening doors that no man could open or shut. He's used bad brothers, a famine, a scorned woman, dreams, and even Joseph's own untimely words to move him exactly where He wanted him, geographically and spiritually. Joseph has been in Egypt at least thirteen years at this point and God had required him to work hard and faithfully while withstanding terrible temptations.

Now, he must look forward, not back. Forward to seven years of preparation for a famine...forward to fruitfulness in the land of his affliction. God did not remove him. He taught him to make a lemonade industry in the land of lemons. We will never know what it was like to be Joseph, accused and misunderstood, except by the Spirit and our own experiences in the Lord. A couple thousand years later, another afflicted man wrote, *'In everything give thanks' 1 Th 5.18*, because you never know what the Lord is up to!

But what WAS the Lord up to? Was Joseph's promotion to *second man in Egypt* the zenith of God's plans and dealings in his life? Was God now resting from all His labor in Joseph's soul, having raised up His man just to administrate the next fourteen years of plenty and famine? Or was there an even higher purpose?

The Gift of a Bad Conscience

About nine years later and two hundred miles to the north, ten brothers and their forlorn, aging father were feeling the harsh effects of a two year old famine. Joseph's predictions were coming to pass, and he was beginning to sell the grain he had stored during seven record-breaking years of harvest. By the time Reuben, Judah and the boys began the journey to Egypt to buy food, 22 years had gone by since they sold their little brother to a band of slave-traders. They had not forgotten, but certainly had repressed the memory and conscience of their horrible crime against Joseph and father Jacob. God had waited this long to reveal his *real* plan for Joseph's life.

Who could truly comprehend the thoughts and emotions that shot through Joseph when he recognized his ten brothers standing in line to buy grain? When they bowed down to him in the marketplace, the Bible simply says that Joseph *'remembered his dreams about them' Ge 42.9*. Then, when he threw them in jail for three days, accusing them of spying, an avalanche of guilt and regret came down on their heads. *They said to one another, "Surely we are being punished because of our brother. We saw how distressed he was when he pleaded with us for his life, but we would not listen; that's why this distress has come upon us." Ge 42.21*

Many people go longer than 22 years without their conscience overwhelming them with an unresolved sin or debacle in their life. Sometimes, in His magnificent wisdom, God allows a sin to incubate in our heart even for years, only to make it hatch with stinging pain, forcing it up through unexpected circumstances, our conscience springing to life. When we realize there's no way out, we're ready to do business with God.

Fear is often associated with secret sins of the past, and *'fear involves torment' 1 Jn 4.18*. The brothers' greatest fear was coming upon them—that their father would find out the truth. They thought they were visiting Egypt just to buy some corn. They hadn't had to deal with the *Joseph issue* for all those years. Little did they know that the harsh, Egyptian-speaking Governor was their little brother and that he understood every word they said! God had brought them to Egypt to give them the most expensive gift of their lives, or anyone's life – outrageous! forgiveness – and it would come through the very person against whom they had sinned.

> *...now it was time to face their fears and be liberated by the awesome power of forgiveness.*

The Most Expensive Gift of All

The man Joseph is the most profound *type* of Jesus Christ in all of scripture. The next few chapters of Genesis (43-45) make it seem like Joseph is playing with his guilt-ridden brothers like a cat plays with a mouse. I used to read it and think, 'My, my Joseph. Lighten up. Give the guys a break. You seem so mean and distant.' But Joseph, like Christ Jesus, was being driven by the unseen power and leading of the Holy Spirit. He was testing the brothers to see if they had *really changed.* For years they had been living with a conscience full of dread. But now it was time to face their fears and be liberated by the awesome power of forgiveness. To bring them there, Joseph remained unrecognizable for a time, speaking harshly to them. One preacher said, *'Before you know Christ as your friend, you must meet Him as your enemy.'*

> Judge not the Lord by feeble sense,
> But trust Him for His grace
> Beneath a frowning Providence
> There hides a smiling face.

In the climactic scene of this drama, Joseph (like Jesus) hid himself and wept for love and pain over his estranged brothers. Finally, when he could bear it no more, and convinced of their sincere grief over the past, he threw everyone else out of the room and cried, *'I am your brother, Joseph, whom you sold into Egypt!'* Ge 45.4. He had every human reason to take vengeance on His own people who had betrayed him. *'But God, who is rich in mercy, and because of His great love for us'* withheld His judgment and extended **outrageous!** forgiveness to us. Joseph's years of pain and waiting were preparation *to forgive the unforgivable.* The God of all grace had taken 22 hard years to work the vindication and anger out of Joseph's soul, so he could be used to bestow forgiveness to people who did not deserve it. He absolutely, completely, unreservedly, outrageously forgave his brothers and insisted that they forgive themselves saying, *'Do not be distressed or angry with yourselves for selling me here, because it was to save lives that God sent me ahead of you'* Gen 45:5.

Joseph's years of pain and waiting were preparation to forgive the unforgivable.

We've all heard the Scripture—it's become almost a cliché—*you reap what you sow.* But think. Have you reaped *everything* you've sown? Joseph (and you) have been prepared to help undeserving people to NOT reap what they've sown. Because as true as is the sowing & reaping law, there's a greater law—*mercy triumphs over judgment.* Jesus and Joseph had every right to not forgive. To insist on their betrayers reaping a nasty harvest. But God—who is rich in mercy—trained Jesus and Joseph and you and me to make an Outrageously powerful Sound from Heaven. The Sound of Outrageous! Forgiveness. I will grant you that there are important techniques and teachings for the effective use of the prophetic ministry. But without the Sound of His Voice becoming the sound of *your* voice, even good technique can fall short.

When Jesus forgives you, there is no holding back, no second-guessing, and no secret anger in Him toward you. Shaming and emotional manipulation have 'leverage' and can coerce people to do many things out of fear or performance, but they have *no spiritual power* – that is, they will not move anyone toward the Presence or Kingdom of God. *'The anger of man does not produce God's righteousness' James 1.20.* Forgiveness is the most expensive gift in all time and eternity, because it cost the most. It cost God His Son's life. It is also the most powerful weapon in the universe, because it can destroy the power and addiction of sin. *'The weapons of our warfare (*like forgiveness*) are not of human power, but are mighty in God to the pulling down of strongholds.'* Forgiveness is total, or it is not forgiveness. The story of Joseph is a **prophecy** of how God, through Jesus Christ, has forgiven us. *'Everybody out of this room! I want to be alone with my brothers so I can forgive them and set them free from guilt and shame.'* Joseph's willingness to wait and test his brothers turned out to be an incredible act of love and proved that his forgiveness was total. The Lord not only wants us to BE forgiven but to KNOW we are forgiven—completely. He also knows that forgiven people are forgiving people.

Most human beings are puzzled, if not frustrated, by the old adage, *forgive and forget.* I'll forgive, but how can I forget that someone spit in my face, abused me, forsook me, betrayed me? Fortunately, God is not our preacher-sermonizer, He's our example. Our Dad doesn't have a bad memory; He can remember details you've long forgotten. But when it comes to the sins He's forgiven, He *chooses* to not remember. With God, forgetting is a choice. *'I am He who blots out your transgressions for My own sake; and I will not remember your sins' Isa 43:25.* He doesn't accuse, hold a grudge, or say, 'I knew you'd do it again' when our sins are under the Blood. That's our assignment – to choose to forget. It took God twenty-two years to teach Joseph that one.

'Forgetting is not a pill you're taking, It's a choice you just keep making'

'Jesus would not entrust himself to them, for he knew all men. He did not need man's testimony about man, for he knew what was in a man' John 2:24-25. Jesus faced reality. He knew how men thought and of what they were capable. He knew the wickedness of some and the weakness of others. He knew their dispositions, their designs, and their tendencies to cave in under pressure. He knew His own disciples were capable of falling asleep in His hour of need. But He didn't let it stop Him from forgiving. He's not forgetful, He just decides to not remember. He didn't entrust Himself to people, because that kind of trust was reserved for His Father. But He gave of Himself in love and mercy. He was brought to the 'alone place' of being totally forsaken of His friends, the angels, and even His Father, so He could show us how to think and live and give when the heat is on. The alone place—with God. The greatest place to be, the hardest place to get to.

He had to go to where all he had was God.

Our friend Joseph? He could not literally forget all that had happened to him. But God helped him become more interested in the restoration of his brothers than in what they had done to him. To help them, he chose to not remember their sins against him. Whether Joseph had asked Him to or not, Father had certainly taken over his life, down to the gory details. But he had to suffer the shock of seeing how frail and sinful other people were – even at his own expense. First he had to face it, then forget it. *'This one thing I do, forgetting what lies behind' Phil 3.13.* Joseph's real Master was showing him he could not go back home to what was comfortable. He had to go to where all he had was God. That's the only place—the only time—we discover what the Lord is really like. I think sometimes God doesn't want us to like our surroundings too much — *at home is in Him.*

I used to think that the story of Joseph's life was about me. And certainly, there are amazing and wonderful parallels between the believer's life and Joseph's. But now I know that Joseph is about Jesus, and that I'm more like his ten rascal brothers. I have a Brother who's been promoted to Governor, and if I'll hang in there with Him, He's ready to restore me completely and say, *'I am Jesus your Brother, who you rejected and sold. But it was God who sent Me before you to save many lives, and to forgive you and bless you and restore you. Let's live and walk together in the land –and where I guide, I'll provide.'*

When I can make that sound to other people, I'm starting to sound like God.

The Sound of Your Voice Series #1

Chapter 7: Joseph's Destiny
or
What Prophetic People Need to Know
or
It Really IS About a Relationship

I have five kids. Grown up now, with responsibilities, dreams, and much work to do. There was a day when their only responsibility was to obey me. But now, I have the delight of enjoying friendship with them, and being blessed by their own life experiences. I'm glad they respect me as their dad, but even more glad that they are happy and free and moving in some of the prayers I prayed for them years ago. Ha! I'm finding that all those Proverbs about obedient children being the glory and delight of their parents are true. After years of pain, was Joseph a delight to Jacob, or what?

No doubt, God is God, and we're not. But being made in His image and living on His earth, much of life and Creation is intended to teach us Who God is and how He planned things to work. As the Ultimate Dad with a Son, He intends our relationships with our kids to teach us how He thinks and how He feels. Yes, feels. He is a Person. He has emotions. He created our emotions and, like Him, He wants us to learn to use and control them. Yes again.

"A wise son is the glory (delight) of his father." We get a big clue as to what God is up to. God's goal for me is not to be a rule-keeper, but a mature son—even a friend—who wants to do it Dad's way because I love Him and His ways, and because He likes to do it with me. By the time Joseph's brothers showed up in Egypt, Joseph was ready to sound like God, to act like a Father.

What about the Rules?

"The law was our school teacher to lead us until Christ came. But now that faith in Christ has come, we no longer need the law as our school teacher" Galatians 3:24-25. Does this nullify or even depreciate the necessity of an obedient heart? Certainly not. I hope my kids continue to brush their teeth and stop at red lights and behave lawfully. But now they do it because they see the value of what I taught them, not because they're worried about a spanking. They love what dad taught them, because dad's ways (hopefully!) made them ready for healthy relationships and success and happiness.

In a magnificent Old Testament glimpse into the New, Jeremiah spoke of why Messiah was coming. *"This is the new covenant I will make with the people, says the LORD. I will put my laws in their minds, and I will write them on their hearts" Jer 31:3.* What an idea!

Israel already had a covenant with God, which included the Ten Commandments. Who thought any more laws or wisdom were needed for life? But Jeremiah spoke of a *new* covenant that was on the way. The very thought of something coming to supersede—even replace—what they already had probably was considered heresy at the time. But God had a Plan. Dad had a Dream. And it wasn't to control His kids with rules. It was to have sons and daughters and friends who would see things His way from the inside, not imposed from the outside.

But kids actually love to live life by rules. Rules, as irritating and constricting as they can be, make life simple. The borders are easy to see, and make kids feel secure, because they know somebody is in charge, and so they feel safe. The Apostle said, *"The purpose of the rules is love from a*

...we will never be God, but God's dream is that we'll think and live like Him. And sound like Him.

pure heart". Even if kids fight them, they love rules and the peace that comes with them. Moments without rules are fun, but life without rules feels very insecure to a child. If there are good laws, life feels secure and safe from bullies. But there is an end game for the rules.

God trains us with rules so that His rules are in our hearts, not so that we can use them like missiles at other people. Hearing and obeying His commandments will eventually lead to deeper love for people, and help you to speak His Truths with grace. So God, in His own Genius way, puts His rules *inside our hearts.* OK, I'll say it again—we will never be God, but God's dream is that we'll think and live like Him. And sound like Him.

So the Ten Commandments are good. Obeying them is better. *Having His rules actually engraved into my thinking is the best.* I hope my son still brushes his teeth. I hope my daughter is honest with her money. I expect that my twins will speak with respect to their wives when they marry. But now they're not obeying rules, they're walking through life with obedience built in. Now, they do the rules because they're embedded in their minds. And their relationship with me is a joy, because love has been built on a foundation of obedience, and healthy relationship and friendship is the tasty, juicy fruit. Is it too good to be true that this is the way God wants it with us?

By the time Joseph's language school was over, he had spent so much time alone with God that he actually had a relationship with Him. He was a New Covenant guy living in Old Covenant times. God wasn't any more worried about him obeying than I am about my kids obeying. He had obedience *built in.* And as a prophet, he had no need to press his (formerly) disgusting brothers with commandments or shame. He shocked them with surprising optimism from Heaven and even told them to stop shaming themselves. Their consciences had done the convicting work, already. This is required understanding for prophetic ministers.

Obedience is essential for children. But compared to the surpassing value of friendship and counsel and communication with dad, obedience can be over-rated. Every son who wants to make the Sound of God to desperate human beings must see that we start with obedience, but it leads to relationship.

I have often used the phrase, "The Lord used me," when speaking of ministry or just giving God's love to others. But no more. I don't "use" my kids. I am delighted that they communicate with me, do things with me, help me, receive my help, etc. I don't want to use anybody. And I don't think the Lord uses His kids, either. Almighty & Sons, Inc. Now that's doing Kingdom business together. That's relationship. That's what Christianity is all about. Now, Joseph the prophet could

You Can Have This

Great theory, yes? But how do you get there, especially when finances, relationships, and 401K's are falling apart before your very eyes? Somebody told me once that the Bible was a handbook on how to live right and to know God. But then I started figuring out that the Lord is not a toy to be put together on Christmas morning by following the directions. He is a Person. A living, moving Person that relates to other persons. He's a God who is a King who is a Dad who is a Friend who is a Lover. Like any relationship, it moves from instructions and rules, to a mature relationship.

> *I have often declared that my Christianity was about relationship, but lived and preached like a rule monger.*

It's not about avoiding DIS-obedience, it's about knowing Him and hearing His Voice and loving to respond with a Yes. Jesus never disobeyed, but even He had to learn to hear His Dad as a Man on earth. It's elementary to obey the basic rules. It's advanced Kingdom to walk through the trials with obedience embedded into your heart. He is our example of developing a relationship with God. He stubbed His toes, ate olives, played as a boy, and was subject to His parents. By the time He was thirty, He was walking in a mature relationship with His (our!) Father. God was so impressed He ripped the sky open and told everyone, *"This is my beloved Son, who greatly pleases Me."*

"Find out what pleases the Lord" (Ephesians 5.10). The Rules are like the "brush your teeth / eat your veggies / go to bed" level of a relationship with God. Essential, but not yet mature. But once you get the basics down—*ha! I suppose we never get it down perfectly*—then it's time for Relationship to grow. Forgive-ness happens in a moment. Finding out what Dad really likes takes a while. There is a 'finding out.' It's not your goal as a mom or dad to order your kids around with rules forever, though you need to at first. Your goal is a happy, healthy, work-and-play-together relationship that will last as long as you're on the planet. Only difference with God is that His relationship plans with us are more like forever.

Like father, like son. Isn't that how God developed the prophet Joseph? It wasn't just for us to admire, but to emulate. I have often declared that my Christianity was about relationship, but lived and preached like a rule monger. But the older I get, the more I see it really is supposed to be a relationship with the Lord. Just one more time—There's no doubt you and I are not God. Neither is there doubt that God has been working on you and me to think and see and love like He does. Isn't that what being a Christian is about?

Anybody can quote God. Few sound like Him. Those who do will make an impact.

Ask Joseph.

The Sound of Your Voice Series #1

Bob Nolan

Bob Nolan found his redemption in Jesus Christ during the Jesus Movement, which swept the world over forty years ago. A self-acknowledged *casualty of the late sixties,* he began his ministry training in northern California and was ordained in 1975.

After completing his B.A. in Biblical Studies at Simpson College in San Francisco (now in Redding, CA), he has served in the Body of Christ as a pastor, teacher, prophetic minister, and worship leader. Bob is the founder and director of **Bible Briefings**—*Prophetic Teaching Ministries.*

Now, in the 21st Century, he is part of another sweeping move of the Holy Spirit in the earth. His "Prophetic Coaching" ministry has trained leaders and saints to move effectively in the Lord's power, "not in word only, but in demonstration of the Spirit."

Bob is an *interpreter of God* to those who want to follow Christ. Ministering in the United States and internationally, his incisive prophetic gifts and words of wisdom call individuals to their destiny in Christ. Believers are encouraged to see God, the Kingdom, and each other by the Holy Spirit.

The Sound of Your Voice Series #1

Welcome to Bible Briefings!

As the Apostle John said, "Jesus came to interpret and explain God to us" (see John 1.18). The heartbeat and purpose of our work is to *"interpret God to human beings."*

Founded and directed by Bob Nolan, Bible Briefings is a teaching and equipping ministry. Bible Briefings draws on many years of pastoral experience, along with prayer and gifts of the Holy Spirit, to serve the Lord and His people in the following ways.

1. *Bible Briefings, a monthly teaching newsletter*, is designed to furnish you with timely scriptural studies, pertinent to your personal walk with the Lord Jesus.

2. *Church / men's retreats* incorporate ministry for character development, prophetic insights, and personal prayer. These weekend meetings, lasting 2-4 days, have proven effective with men's groups or an entire congregation.

3. *Honduras, Taiwan, China short-term missions* is a teaching and prophetic ministry intensive for leaders and churches in Central America and Southeast Asia. Our vision is to open doors for others as the Lord makes the way, so please let us know if you would like to be involved through prayer, training or missions support.

4. *Adjunct faculty, a service to Bible Colleges / Training Centers*, provides short-term (2-4 weeks) Biblical and theological training for colleges, discipleship training, and ministry equipping centers.

5. ***Life Coaching*** encourages you, your family, or your business to move forward in the purpose for which you were designed. We combine a Personality Profile evaluation, twenty-five years of counseling experience, and proven Biblical principles, and a positive approach to encourage growth and success in your life. We also provide office staff training for service and leadership skills. We coach in person, by telephone, or on the Internet.

6. ***Prophetic Training*** equips the saints by passing on knowledge and experience in the specific service to which a believer is called. Only God can give the gift, but every gift is given to be stewarded and developed by faith, obedience, and use. The Holy Spirit wants those who operate in these ministries to mature in their effective use of their gifts. **The "prophetic training" ministry is to help equip those with prophetic inclinations by coaching them in the *knowledge, experience, and effective use* of the ministry of prophecy.** Seminars with personal teaching and application training are available through Bible Briefings.

If you would like to join our mailing list, schedule a Bible Briefings event, or order more books, please refer to the contact information following.

Bob Nolan

Bible Briefings—Prophetic Teaching Ministries

PO Box 100
Ontario, California. 91762

Email: Briefings1@gmail.com
Phone: 707-295-0675

"Interpreting God to human beings"

www.ingramcontent.com/pod-product-compliance
Lightning Source LLC
Chambersburg PA
CBHW060854050426
42453CB00008B/971